MORE MARVELLOUS
CANADIANS!

Hysterically Historical Rhymes

GORDON SNELL

With caricatures by
AISLIN

McArthur & Company
Toronto

National Library of Canada Cataloguing in Publication

Snell, Gordon
More marvellous Canadians! :
hysterically historical rhymes / Gordon Snell ;
with caricatures by Aislin.

ISBN 1–55278–313–8

1. Celebrities—Canada—Poetry. 2. Humorous poetry, English.
3. Canadian wit and humor, Pictorial. I. Aislin II. Title.

PR6069.N44M67 2002   821'.914   C2002-903572-4

Cover Illustration by *AISLIN*
Layout, Design and Electronic Imaging by *MARY HUGHSON*
Printed and Bound in Canada by
TRANSCONTINENTAL PRINTING INC.

The publisher would like to acknowledge the financial support of the
Government of Canada through the Book Publishing Industry Development
Program (BPIDP) and the Canada Council for our publishing activities. The
publisher further wishes to acknowledge the financial support of the Ontario
Arts Council for our publishing program.

10 9 8 7 6 5 4 3 2

McArthur & Company

Toronto

322 KING STREET WEST, SUITE 402, TORONTO, ONTARIO, CANADA M5V 1J2

These rhymes are for Maeve
Whom I love and bless
For our life of joy and happiness.

GS

All these sketches,
From front to back,
Are for Connor, Morgan,
And little Jack.

A

MORE MARVELLOUS
CANADIANS!

Hysterically Historical Rhymes

Contents

THE NEWFOUNDLAND DOG

*(Its origins are uncertain, but in the past two hundred years
the Newfoundland has established itself as a much loved
and much admired breed in Canada and many other countries.
Its heroic exploits and friendly nature have earned it
a high profile in history and in literature)*

Some claim these dogs were brought here first
By some fierce Viking crew,
While others said they've been cross-bred
With wolves and mastiffs too.

Whatever ancestors they had,
Canadians understand
There is indeed no canine breed
To match the Newfoundland.

With massive head and jet-black coat
This handsome heavyweight
Sturdy and strong, will lope along
With steady, rolling gait.

The dogs were kept on fishing boats
To dive for drowning men:
Into the deep they'd bravely leap
And bring them back again.

Napoleon one night had gone
And fallen off a boat.
This dog, for sure, crying *"Au secours!"*
Kept Bonaparte afloat.

The hearts of those this dog has saved
With gratitude are brimming –
Though several more he dragged ashore
Had simply gone out swimming.

The playwright J.M. Barrie
Put his dog in *Peter Pan*,
And praise he earns from Robert Burns
For being a "gentleman".

When *his* dogs played together
They made Charles Dickens laugh,
And Byron penned for his Best Friend
A noble epitaph.

If there were Dog Olympics
Gold medals they would bring
And stand up proud as all the crowd
Oh, Canada would sing!

MARGUERITE DE ROBERVAL
(Sixteenth Century)

(In 1542, Jean Francois de Roberval sailed with three ships to found a settlement in New France. His niece, Marguerite, went with him – and so did her lover, as a stowaway. When they were found out, her uncle marooned them on the uninhabited Isle of Demons – probably Fogo Island – off the coast of Newfoundland)

A tragic tale of Boy Meets Gal
Faced Marguerite de Roberval.
Her uncle, anxious to advance
The colony they called New France,
Sailed with a group two hundred strong
And asked his niece to come along.

Such is the power of L'Amour,
Her lover also joined the tour.
He stowed away – oh, how romantic! –
Until they'd crossed the whole Atlantic.

After two months the little band
Were off the coast of Newfoundland.
They stopped to get supplies in store,
And then the lovers sneaked ashore.
They fished for salmon every day,
And spent the nights in amorous play.

Marguerite's uncle, finding out,
Began to rage and stamp about.
He cried: "Oh, Marguerite, what shame
You've brought upon the family name!
Now I shall give you both short shrift –
Tomorrow you'll be cast adrift."

In a deserted island bay
The crew left them, and rushed away:
A superstition of the seamen's
Gave it the name The Isle of Demons.

There they were both abandoned then
With Marguerite's servant, Damienne.
Her uncle left her with a gun
And so some hunting could be done.
They lived upon the game they'd shoot,
And birds' eggs, berries, fish and fruit.

They built a cabin too, and there
They sheltered from the chill night air
And listened to the haunting cries
Of strange birds echo in the skies.

Hoping for ships, they kept their eyes on
The ocean and the far horizon.
Month after month went slowly past
And still they saw no sail or mast.

The lovers had each other – though
Poor Damienne felt a bit de trop.

There was some consolation, maybe,
When Marguerite produced a baby.
Its father had grown ill, and died;
But Marguerite the fates defied,
And so the three of them went on
Till nine more months had come and gone.

Then Damienne and the child died too –
Alone now, what could Marguerite do?
One more full year she struggled through
Till Breton fishermen arrived,
Amazed that Marguerite survived.

Back home with them to France she'd sail
And there she told her wondrous tale,
And countless readers were entranced
To hear the story she advanced.

She'd shown what human beings could stand
Simply by living off the land.
It was a lesson that Champlain
Used when he sailed to that terrain:
He owed success at Port Royal
To Marguerite de Roberval.

JOHN JEWITT
(1784 – 1821)

(In 1803, John Jewitt was a young armourer aboard the trading ship Boston, when it sailed into Nootka Sound, Vancouver Island. His encounter with the local ruler, Chief Maquinna, was the start of two years in which he lived with the Chief and his people, learned their language and adopted their culture. He wrote a book about his years there, called A Narrative of the Adventures and Sufferings of John R. Jewitt *which became a popular success and made Chief Maquinna's name famous)*

When first the trader *Boston* came
To visit Nootka Sound
The Captain was delighted
With the welcome that they found.

When Chief Maquinna came aboard
With salmon as a gift
He got a rifle in return
And his response was swift.

He shot a lot of ducks to give
The Captain as a token,
But then remarked: "This gun has failed –
You see, the lock has broken."

The Captain fumed and thought he lied –
And Chief Maquinna knew it.
The gun was given for repair
To armourer John Jewitt.

Next night, Chiefs came aboard to feast;
Below, John Jewitt waited.
He came on deck to find the crew
Had been decapitated.

An axe caught John a savage blow –
He fell down then and there,
And coming to, his eyes were held
By Chief Maqinna's glare.

The Chief asked: "Will you be my slave
And fix our knives and guns?"
John saw the knife he brandished
And replied: "I'll start at once!"

John Jewitt took to tribal life
And learned the language too,
And soon between the Chief and John
A curious friendship grew.

John wrote with care and sympathy
Of how they lived their lives,
Made blades and fish-hooks for the Chiefs
And bracelets for their wives.

He watched the ceremonials:
When gatherings took place
It took the Chief at least an hour
To decorate his face.

Two years went by, and then one day
The Chief took John aside.
He told him: "Now you're one of us,
It's time you had a bride."

John Jewitt wasn't very keen
But when the Chief said: "*Will* you?
Please answer *Yes*, John – otherwise
I fear we'll have to kill you!"

So John agreed, and off they went
With gifts, in two canoes.
They visited another tribe
So John a bride could choose.

Maqinna praised him to the skies
And said: "His worth is real,
Although he might be rather white
And looks just like a seal!"

A lovely girl of seventeen
Became John Jewitt's wife.
"And now," Maqinna said, "It's time
You took our way of life."

His old clothes off, John wrapped himself
In woven cloths instead,
And painted face and body too
With patterns black and red.

With his new wife he had a son,
And then, one fateful day,
A trading ship from Boston
Came sailing to the bay.

Maqinna said: "I'll go aboard –
No harm they will intend
If John writes me a letter now
To say that I'm his friend."

John claimed he'd written glowingly,
But really he attested
The Chief had led the massacre
And he should be arrested.

Maqinna when he went aboard
Thought peace and friendship reigned
But knew the truth when soon he found
That he was bound and chained.

When finally a deal was done
John Jewitt came aboard;
Maqinna was magnanimous,
The treachery ignored.

The two talked long into the night
And then upon the morrow
They parted with a fond embrace
And many tears of sorrow.

John's wife went back to join her tribe –
Their son was left alone;
But Chief Maqinna had declared
He'd raise him as his own.

John settled in New England –
The book he wrote, what's more,
He piled into a horse and cart
And peddled door to door.

It was a popular success,
And found on many a shelf.
He even made a play of it
In which he starred himself.

THOMAS HALIBURTON
(1796 – 1865)

*(Born in Windsor, Nova Scotia, Haliburton became a barrister
and a member of the provincial assembly. He went on to be a
Supreme Court judge, and to make his name as the creator of
Sam Slick the Clockmaker, whose sayings and encounters were
a satirical commentary on Canadian life and times)*

Few men had views more sure and certain
Than Thomas Chandler Haliburton,
And from those views he would not budge
As politician or as judge.

He was a Loyalist through and through
And thought the Colonies he knew
Would only thrive, poor fragile things,
If tied to Britain's apron-strings.

But they should also get the chance
In British circles to advance,
With equal rights and expectations
And not as distant poor relations.

His views, though forthright and intense,
Would have no greater audience

Than those of any other Tory's –
Until he started writing stories.

Now it was Haliburton's notion
To write them for the *Nova Scotian*.
Sam Slick, his comical creation,
Gained him the readers' acclamation.

A Yankee salesman, peddling clocks,
Sam Slick can be unorthodox,
And as he travels all around
His views he'll readily expound.

An English Squire is the recipient
Of thoughts outrageous, and percipient.
Sam boasts Americans have reckoned
There's cash in every hour and second.

Blue Noses, as he calls the locals,
Are just a bunch of idle yokels.
At work or industry they balk –
They'd rather drink and smoke and talk.

Their province, if they'd only see,
Could flourish in prosperity
If they'd just emulate the Yanks –
A view that gets Sam little thanks.

Blue Noses aren't the only folks
To be the butt of Sam Slick's jokes:
"For *John Bull*, no name could be fitter:
A vain, bull-headed, vicious critter.
Such blown-up self-conceit he has,
He's like a walking bag of gas!"

Yet Sam reserved his worst attacks
For citizens of Halifax.
He said, when asked what view he'd take:
"I'll tell you when the town's awake –
It's just as lively and pulsating
As bears when they are hibernating!"

For Haliburton's fans, the essence
Of Sam Slick was his smart expressions.
There's many a phrase he gets the credit
For being the very first who said it.
The "Upper Crust" is one such term,
And "Early birds will get the worm."

So Haliburton joined the lists
Of pioneering humorists.
Sam Slick became, the swaggering feller,
The first Canadian Best-Seller.

SIR WILFRID LAURIER
(1841 – 1919)

(Ottawa's grandiose Chateau Laurier and Sir Wilfrid Laurier
University are just two of the places that commemorate the first
French Canadian to become Prime Minister. Born in St-Lin near
Montreal, Laurier practised law before moving into politics.
His tenacity combined with his talent for compromise helped him
win four elections in a row, as he pursued his vision of
Canada as an independent sovereign nation)

Even at school, young Wilfrid saw
The fascination of the Law.
He studied it with flair and skill
And graduated from McGill.

Then, practising in Montreal,
To politics he felt the call,
And his commitment would be huge
Once he had joined the Parti Rouge,
Whose politics the Catholic Church
Strongly endeavoured to besmirch.

Now Laurier began to show
The skills that made his stature grow:
The talent for conciliation
That strengthened the Canadian nation.

So, ummm, does this like mean that the 21st Century belongs to Canada?
MERDE..!
CANADA
CINQ • FIVE DOLLARS
3.10 US
3.10 US
AISLIN

He calmed the Church's opposition
Towards the Liberal tradition,
And in the party he would make
A special friend of Edward Blake.
Later, when Blake stepped down as head,
He wanted Laurier instead.

The Liberals had always made
A great commitment to Free Trade.
Tariffs, they said, no part should play
In commerce with the U.S.A.

This policy of Reciprocity
The Tories savaged with ferocity.
The voters seemed to hate it too,
So Laurier knew what to do.

It would be very wise – he sensed it –
If Liberals also were against it:
A U-Turn which would prove no blunder –
He'd stolen all the Tories' thunder!

When Manitoba planned new rules
To further special Catholic schools
He said it would be very rash
To launch into a head-on clash.
A subtler course he would advise:
The "sunny ways" of compromise.

With criticism now deflected
He duly got himself elected.
Well might the gloomy Tories cower:
He stayed for fifteen years in power.

Handsome and suave and debonair
He spoke with eloquence and flair.
The opposition he disarmed
And many ladies smoothly charmed.
Letters of love especially
He wrote to *Dearest Emilie*

But most of all, his mind would see
The nation Canada could be.

During his rule he would be seeing
Two provinces come into being.
That status was conferred upon
Alberta and Saskatchewan,
And there he'd add, by immigration,
A million to the population.

The Yukon Territory was named
Where many a Gold Rush stake was claimed.
For railways too he went full tilt:
Not one, but two, he wanted built.

His great achievement, he insisted,
Was in the pressures he resisted.

He stopped America encroaching,
Frustrating those intent on poaching:
One U.S. leader even planned
To annex all Canadian land.

But it was vital, Laurier knew,
To block demands from Britain too.
His greatest triumph there would be
At Queen Victoria's Jubilee.

He led the great Procession through
And gladly took a knighthood too.
He praised the Empire with such pride
The British thought: "He's on our side."

But when the Conference was held
And closer ties they tried to weld,
Binding the whole Canadian nation
In what was called Consolidation,
The new Sir Wilfrid struck a blow
With one emphatic answer: "NO!"

Over the years with him they'd plead
Canadian sovereignty to cede.
But they could wheedle, roar or rant –
Still Laurier would not recant.
The British side, frustrated so,
Called him *The Everlasting NO!*

His NO's in fact gave affirmation
To Canada as sovereign nation,
And as a hero many claimed him:
The *First Canadian* they named him.
His image gazes at us still
From Canada's five dollar bill.

JOSEPH BURR TYRRELL
(1858 – 1957)

(As a scientist with the national Geological Survey, Joseph Burr Tyrrell made many long and perilous journeys mapping the bleak northern regions of the Canadian wilderness. He made a great contribution to the development of the mining industry, but his most celebrated discovery was the huge bed of fossilized dinosaur remains near Drumheller in Alberta, where he is commemorated in the popular Royal Tyrrell Museum of Palaeontology)

Joseph Tyrrell as a boy
Would scorn the usual kind of toy.
Instead, he'd hike all day to find
Insects and bugs of every kind.
He even risked his parents' wrath
By keeping crayfish in the bath.

The outdoor life with lots of hiking
Was very much to Joseph's liking
And so it seemed extremely logical
To join the Survey Geological.

The Barren Ground he travelled through
By foot and snowshoe and canoe;
Thousands of miles of desolation
Brought cold, fatigue and near-starvation.

Once when a polar bear was shot
The hungry party ate the lot,
And then three hundred miles in all
They had to stagger, walk and crawl:
They took a month to make their way
To Churchill town on Hudson Bay.

But even when he neared collapse
Tyrrell continued making maps –
Maps that would lead him on to find
Coal, ore and gold that could be mined.

One find that made his senses quiver
Was on the banks of Red Deer River.
There in the cliff he was surprised
To see a large skull, fossilized –
A dinosaur who lived, we know,
Some sixty million years ago.

As down the cliff he made the climb
He said: "It's been a long, long time
Here in Alberta waiting for us:
I'll call it the *Albertosaurus*."

The creature must have had great strength
At nearly thirty feet in length,
But this was just one creature's fossil –
The total find was just colossal.

Tyrannosaurus Rex was there
And scientists could also stare
At hollow eyes and bony chops
Of *Duckbills* and *Triceratops*.

This richest graveyard in the world
Had nests where fossil babies curled
And eggs, and skeletons galore
Of thirty kinds of dinosaur –
A treasure trove was lying here
And he had been its pioneer.

Seventeen years saw Tyrrell staying
In geological surveying.
He then took up a new career:
Consultant mining engineer.

The Klondike Gold Rush had begun:
Among the seekers, he was one,
Living the life of gaudy, gritty
And raw, rambunctious Dawson City.

In his long life his fame grew big –
He seemed to know just where to dig.
By mining companies employed
He saw that they were overjoyed
When he found minerals and ore.
Their wealth – and his – grew more and more.

Yet Joseph Tyrrell's greatest claim
In history, to lasting fame
Is the Museum with his name,
Where half a million come each year
To learn, to marvel and to peer
At these giant beasts who used to roam
Supreme in their Alberta home.

ODES
for
Wampum

PAULINE JOHNSON
(1861 – 1913)

*(Pauline Johnson was born on the Six Nations Reserve near
Brantford, Ontario, the daughter of a Mohawk chief and his
English-born wife. Her mother taught her to love poetry,
and she began to write poems herself and then to tour
throughout Canada and in the USA and Britain, giving recitals
which drew large and enthusiastic audiences)*

As a child, young Pauline Johnson
Wasn't reading fairy stories –
She was reading *Hiawatha*
Longfellow's great *Hiawatha*,
Got to know the pounding rhythm
Of those long hypnotic verses.

She was also reading Byron,
Keats and Walter Scott and Shakespeare –
Was it really any wonder
Pauline chose to be a poet?

First in magazines she published,
Then brought out her first collection
And *White Wampum* she did call it,
Wampum being a shell-bead necklace.

She was quite a fan of wampums
And the name that she adopted
Which was *Tekahionwake*
(Sounding so much more exotic
Than prosaic *Pauline Johnson*)
Has the meaning, *Double Wampum.*

Pauline wrote of rural idylls,
Twilight and the misty marshland,
Paddling through the river water
Even through the *Laughing Water,*
Telling too the tribal stories
Which her grandfather had told her,
Tales of chieftains and of rituals
And of Indian deprivation.

Poetry she soon discovered
Wasn't making any money
So to make ends meet she started
On a programme of recitals.
She became the *Mohawk Princess,*
Dressed herself in beaded buckskins,
Mocassins and fancy feathers
As she gave her recitations,
Pausing now and then to utter
Loud and startling whoops and war-cries.

Then she'd don another costume:
Evening dress, all white brocaded,
And give further recitations.

How the audiences loved her:
Sentimental and romantic
With an air of tribal mystery
She was lovely and enchanting.

Coast to coast she toured the country,
Twenty times she crossed the country,
Churches, theatres, halls and bar-rooms
Were the scenes where Pauline triumphed –
In the USA and Britain
She was also much applauded.

After years of constant touring
Constant touring and reciting
Pauline settled in Vancouver
Where she heard the many legends
Told by Chief Joe Capilano
All about the Squamish nation.

There her final book was written
Titled *Legends of Vancouver*,
Highly praised for all its insights
Into tribal myths and legends.

And in Stanley Park, Vancouver,
Stands a big grey stone memorial
To honour this Canadian poet
Who believed that all her writings
Made a bridge between two cultures
And made her the *Mohawk Princess*.

REGINALD FESSENDEN
(1866 – 1932)

(Reginald Fessenden was born in Milton, Quebec. He became a brilliant electrical engineer and had hundreds of inventions and patents to his credit. He was the first to succeed in transmitting voice signals by radio waves, though this and his other achievements did not get him the fame he really merited)

Reginald Fessenden must have felt sore –
He deserved a lot more recognition.
He sent words by radio, one year before
Marconi made *his* first transmission.

With Edison, whom he was glad to admire,
A job testing street lights he got,
Then invented a compound to insulate wire
And prevent it from getting too hot.

His volatile temperament sometimes was feared –
He was really not hard to provoke.
He cut quite a dash with his flaming red beard
And the swirl of his flowing black cloak.

At electrical sciences he was a star,
An inventor with genius and flair.

But of all his ambitions the greatest by far
Was to send voices out through the air.

He built a great tower four hundred feet high
To transmit human voices, with luck.
He climbed up inside it, adjustments to try,
But because of his size, he got stuck.

His colleagues – the ones who were not so obese –
Then anxiously climbed up inside.
They stripped him, and smeared
his whole body with grease,
So that down to the ground he could slide.

But the transmitter worked – it sent every word
And with joy the inventor was frantic,
For by radio waves, his voice had been heard
In Scotland, across the Atlantic.

In 1906, on a cold Christmas Eve,
As cargo ships went to and fro
The sailors heard something they couldn't believe:
The first ever Radio Show.

Reginald Fessenden played the violin,
Read the Bible, and sang loud and clear;
And to round off the broadcast he said with a grin:
"Merry Christmas and Happy New Year!"

So many inventions he went on to claim
In Canada, and in the States,
That honestly, Reginald Fessenden's name
Deserves to be there with the Greats.

NELLIE McCLUNG
(1876 – 1951)

(Nellie McClung grew up in Manitoba where she became a teacher, was active in the women's suffrage movement and wrote a best-selling novel. With her pharmacist husband and five children she went to live in Winnipeg, where her forthright campaigning style made her a popular leader and the bane of the Establishment. She was one of the five women in the 'Persons Case', challenging the bizarre law which said that women were not legally 'persons')

We owe much to Nellie McClung,
A campaigner creative and keen:
A battling feminist since she was young,
She transformed the political scene.

In Winnipeg, Nellie was leader
Of a specially formed delegation.
They went to the Premier, hoping he'd heed her
And give votes to the whole population.

The Premier was called Rodmond Roblin
(In fact, he'd the title of Sir.)
And he'd really much rather give votes to a goblin
Than Nellie and people like her.

As she spoke, his brain started to fizz
And he barked: "She is getting my goat.
A hyena in petticoats, that's what she is!
Nice women have no wish to vote."

Dismissed, Nellie said: "We can't wait,
So we'll stage a Mock Parliament then –
And the topical motion we'll choose to debate
Is "Should there be voting for men?"

Nellie spoke in the Premier's voice;
She said: "Men are as noble as kings –
It only unsettles them, having a choice –
Votes would make them uneasy, poor things!"

Her Parliament caused much hilarity
And some furious insults as well.
Her critics attacked her for sneering vulgarity,
Her supporters gave cheers for "Our Nell."

When the Liberals came on the scene
They decided to back Nellie's cause.
Manitoba was first, back in 1916,
To pass new equality laws.

The Assembly burst into song
When the suffrage decision was made.

The women's campaign had been bruising and long
And Nellie had led the crusade.

New battles remained to be fought:
The "Persons Case" soon would arrive.
By the *Famous Five* women the case had been brought,
And Nellie was one of the five.

That victory won, Nellie still didn't rest,
As well as being mother and wife,
For reforms and for justice with zeal and with zest
She campaigned for the rest of her life.

JUDGE JACK SISSONS
1892– 1969)

*(Born in Ontario, Jack Sissons moved in his twenties to
Alberta where he practised law and became a judge.
He championed minority rights and often clashed with the
establishment. At the age of sixty-three he was appointed as the
first judge of the Territorial Court of the Northwest Territories,
where he was revered by the people and often reviled by Ottawa)*

Jack Sissons was delighted
To be posted to the north,
And for a life in Yellowknife
He very soon set forth.

No other judge had territory
Of such gigantic span,
For through one third of Canada
His jurisdiction ran.

He knew that half the people there
Were of the Inuit race
So he set out to learn about
Their culture and their ways.

He thought that justice should be brought
To everybody's door

And so, to try a case, he'd fly
A thousand miles or more.

In bumpy single-engined planes
Judge Sissons used to ride
And cases slight or serious
Impartially he tried:

Adoption, murder, suicide,
And marriage customs too,
As well as fights for hunting rights
And makers of home-brew.

In making known his forthright views
The judge was firm and vocal:
"All must have trial by their peers,
And juries must be local."

And then, in 1962,
The *Duck Case* came along:
A magistrate said shooting ducks
Was, in close season, wrong.

Judge Sissons quashed that verdict
And gave his legal reason:
The Indian Treaties granted rights
To hunt in any season.

Many such landmark verdicts
The northern people saw,
Respecting their traditions
Within the rule of law.

Though many people in his courts
Thought Sissons was their saviour
The bureaucrats were driven bats
By all his bold behaviour.

"Those bright boys down in Ottawa,"
He said, "have set their sights
On full control of everything
Except the Northern Lights!"

Self-government, he always claimed,
Was what the region needed.
At last, two years before he died,
His long campaign succeeded.

Now *Ekoktoegee* was the name
The Inuit called Judge Sissons –
A worthy tribute to his fame:
It means *"the one who listens."*

FAY WRAY
(Born 1907)

*(Alberta-born Fay Wray moved as a child with her family
to California where she soon got parts in movies as an extra and
then in more major roles. She was able to make the transition
from silent films to talkies, and had her big screen success in the
celebrated monster movie,* King Kong *– a role which has tended to
overshadow the many other achievements of her long lifetime)*

Fay Wray was born, as one of six,
In what some cynics call The Sticks.
Near Cardston in Alberta, Fay
First came to see the light of day.

The family moved south, and Fay
Was happy living in L.A.
For that was where the films were made,
The centre of the movie trade.

Just in her teens, Fay Wray was seen
In Westerns on the silent screen:
A winsome heroine, with lots
Of noiseless hooves and silent shots –
Rescued of course, for plots don't vary,
By gallant cowboys on the prairie.

And soon the talent scouts would cast her
With Janet Gaynor, Mary Astor
And other starlets, to be some
Of movies' greats in years to come.

Von Stroheim's *Wedding March* became
The film that launched her into fame.
What's more, it got her off the ground
With a career in films with Sound.

When Talking Pictures first arrived
Not every silent screen star thrived,
For some of them were heard to speak
With voices like a croak or squeak.

But Fay Wray's talking passed the test,
And then she found she was the best
At one sound more than all the rest:
Fay Wray became the *Queen of Scream*,
 The Horror-Movie-Maker's dream!

The movie-goers flocked to see 'em:
The Vampire Bat, *The Wax Museum*,
And many more – the fans, she knew,
Were terrified, and deafened too.

And then her big chance came along
To co-star with the ape, *King Kong*.

That hairy and primeval monster
In filmdom's Hall of Fame ensconced her.

The great adventure story features
An island full of giant creatures
Who lived a million years before us:
Triceratops and Stegosaurus –
All fierce and furious and strong,
But none of them a match for Kong.

The island tribe who kidnap Fay
Give her to Kong as luscious prey.
As fearful in his cave she nestles
The giant ape goes out and wrestles:
No jungle creature there can match him
But humans find a way to catch him.

He's gassed and captured, brought away
And in New York put on display.
But Kong, escaping from his cage,
Goes on a city-wide rampage;
And where is Fay? She's far from calm
Clutched in his tender, hairy palm.

And really, no-one could expect her
To know he's trying to protect her!
Where can Kong go, to flee his fate?
Where else, but up the Empire State?

While Fay is screaming, loud and long,
The planes attack, and conquer Kong.

The movie, when it went on show,
Made millions for the studio.
So hectic then was Fay's career
She made – astonishing to hear –
Eleven movies in one year.

She was a film director's wife
And led a star's luxurious life:
A mansion, cocktails, tea and tennis –
And largely thanks to King Kong's menace.

She went on making films, retired,
Came back, remaining much admired,
Wrote books, and dramas for the stage,
And then at ninety years of age
This star who had her name in lights
Was lobbying for writers' rights.

Alberta's girl had made the grade
In glitzy Hollywood's parade,
And movie fans still love to gape
At Fay and her gigantic ape.

YOUSUF KARSH OF OTTAWA
(1908 – 2002)

(After his family fled from persecution in Armenia, Yousuf Karsh
was sent to Canada in 1924 to join his uncle, a photographer in
Sherbrooke, Quebec. He went to school there, and then began a
career in photography which made his name world-famous)

Oh, what a photogenic scene
Karsh's arrival would have been
In Halifax, aged just sixteen!

He travelled then, on New Year's Day
Up from the docks by horse-drawn sleigh
While bells were tinkling all the way.

The snowbound train trip then was harsh,
But it was joy to Yousuf Karsh,
The young, excited boy who planned
To make his way in this new land.

First with his uncle he would start
To learn the photographic art;
Then down to Boston made the trip
For three more years' apprenticeship.

John Garo, generous and wise,
Taught Yousuf how to use his eyes
To see the shapes, the light and shade
From which a picture would be made.

Garo, to get his portraits right
Would use no artificial light.
Later, in Ottawa, Karsh met
The members of the theatre set,
And watching them at work he knew
Just what electric lights could do.

He boldly thought he'd have a go
At setting up a studio.
It was a struggle to begin
With little money coming in.

His clients had to sit and wait
Upon a cushioned orange-crate.
His secretary, in early stages,
Lent him the cash to pay her wages.

A Drama Festival had been
Pictured by Karsh, in photos seen
In Ottawa's top magazine.

Of many actors, there was one
Who was the Governor General's son.

Karsh asked him if on his behalf
He would request a photograph.

And so the Governor General came
To sit for Karsh, and make his name:
He took a portrait that became
The first to bring him widespread fame.

Then, as his reputation grew
The portrait subjects that he knew
Began to read just like Who's Who.

He photographed tycoons galore
And kings and princes by the score,
Popes, Presidents and politicians,
And hordes of actors and musicians.

One picture won him world-wide praise:
Sir Winston Churchill, stern of gaze,
Poses with grim determination
To suit the leader of his nation.

There's no cigar seen anywhere:
Why? Karsh didn't want it there –
So reaching with his finger-tips
He plucked it out from Churchill's lips.
Could that bold move, we wonder now,
Account for Churchill's furrowed brow?

Pablo Casals he bravely shows
In startling back-to-camera pose.
Glenn Gould, although it might seem daft,
Said that before being photographed,
A new grand piano must be hired
Tuned perfectly, as he desired.

Karsh photographed Lord Beaverbrook
Who saw the picture that he took
And said: "Now Karsh, you have surprised me –
I think you have immortalised me!"
("But were you wise," a friend would chortle,
"Dear Karsh, to make that man immortal?")

Karsh was enthralled, he'd always state,
By what made men and women great –
That quality, that special glow,
Was what he always tried to show –
And with that talent, it is true,
He joined the ranks of greatness too.

RAYMOND BURR
(1917 – 1993)

*(Raymond Burr was born in New Westminster, BC,
moved south to California and started his acting career at the
Pasadena Playhouse. His first movie role was as a prisoner in*
San Quentin, *and he went on to play the heavy villain in
many films, until the TV series* Perry Mason *and later*
Ironside *made him an international star)*

The burly bulk of Raymond Burr
Loomed on many a movie screen.
His roles in lots of movies were
Villains menacing and mean.

With the Marx Brothers he played
And with *Tarzan* and *Godzilla*.
Serpent of the Nile he made,
And also *Bride of the Gorilla*.

James Stewart's *Rear Window* looked upon
His neighbour, white-haired Raymond Burr.
James wondered where his wife had gone –
Had he done away with her?

Then the audiences saw
Raymond change his villain's stance.

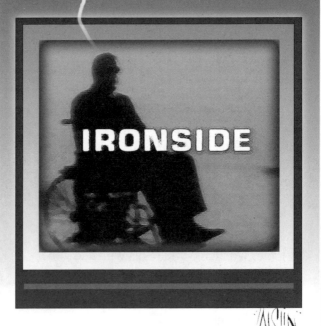

On the right side of the Law
Perry Mason was his chance.

Under his examinations
Guilty witnesses would stumble
As last-minute revelations
Caused the murderer's case to crumble.

Catchy titles marked each case:
The Reckless Romeo was one –
Shooting Star, *Avenging Ace*,
And even *The Notorious Nun*.

While we all saw Perry meet
Each challenge in his forthright fashion,
His assistant Della Street
Surely nursed a secret passion?

With nearly thirty cases tried,
Perry Mason left the screen;
As Detective Ironside
Raymond Burr could now be seen.

Through each story's twists and turns
His wheelchair skilfully he steers.
With sincerity he burns
In every case, for seven years.

Then further film roles he'd assume:
Airplane Two was quite a joke.
In *The Curse of King Tut's Tomb*
He glowered in a purple cloak.

Though film stardom might be fine,
Life held more for Raymond Burr:
He grew orchids, and of wine
He became a connoisseur.

His *Perry* and his *Ironside*
Ensure his memory will not dim.
His partner Robert, when he died,
Named their vineyards after him.

LILI ST. CYR
(1918 – 1999)

(As a young girl, Lili dreamed of being an adventuress, and when she grew up, she certainly had many adventures. She lived the high life, had six marriages and many lovers, and became a celebrated 'stripteaseuse'. For years she was the star of the vaudeville shows at the Gayety Theatre in Montreal, which she called the enchanted city where her dreams became reality)

When Lili St. Cyr cast her spell
The audience gasped: *"Elle est belle!"*
    Her act was exotic
    And highly erotic
Each dance had a story to tell.

As the Queen of the Jungle she shone
Though a head-dress was all she had on.
    As Eve she would grapple
    With a *very* large apple –
As Salome, her veils were soon gone.

Strong men's hearts at her antics would melt:
In one scene, she would strip to her pelt
    And her charms were displayed

As to Buddha she prayed
For the key to her chastity belt!

By the Church she was truly detested
Though their waves of resentment she breasted,
   But to safeguard the city
   The Morals Committee
Contrived to have Lili arrested.

But her critics, the Judge got to know,
Had not even been to the show.
   When three housewives as well
   Said that Lili was swell
The Judge said: "You're quite free to go!"

In the night-clubs and bars she was fêted;
As a true *Femme Fatale* she was rated.
   And on stage they would cheer
   For Lili St. Cyr
And the way that she writhed and gyrated.

NORMAN JEWISON
(Born 1926)

*(Born in Toronto, Norman Jewison joined the Navy in
World War Two, then went to the University of Toronto, and
studied music at the Royal Conservatory. After a spell in London
as an actor and scriptwriter, he joined the CBC and then went
on to become a film director. His many feature films have won
him international fame and over fifty major awards.
He founded the Canadian Film Centre, now a celebrated
training ground and research centre in the cinematic arts)*

Many Canadians make it good
As movie stars in Hollywood
But few who top the billing there
Have sat in the Director's Chair –
And brightest of them all has shone
The name of Norman Jewison.

His earliest success would be
Directing for the CBC.
Work on the *Wayne and Shuster Show*
Made Norman's reputation grow.

Then CBS shows came his way:
He worked with stars like Danny Kaye;

His talents Frank Sinatra knew,
And Harry Belafonte too.

The Judy Garland Show was troubled:
Disaster loomed, and tantrums bubbled,
But Norman Jewison survived
And got two Emmys as he thrived –
And then for Big Screen fame he strived.

His early movies in L.A.
Were comedies with Doris Day.
Then as a triumph on the screen
The *Cincinnati Kid* was seen
With poker-playing Steve McQueen.

And Norman Jewison would then
Turn back to comedy again –
A daunting task it well might seem:
This time the Cold War was his theme.
Could he succeed in making comic
Nuclear bombs and threats atomic?

The Russians are coming, the Russians are coming
Had critics with excitement humming.
What Norman called his *War and Peace*
Had a spectacular release,
For *Pravda* gave a rave review –
The Senate even praised it too!

In many of the films he made
His social conscience was displayed:
The Hurricane – In the Heat of the Night –
Took up the anti-racist fight.

But Hollywood did look askance
At forthright views that he'd advance.
The Vietnam War he would attack
And once he sent his green card back.
But audiences still enjoyed him
So studios once more employed him.

His greatest skills were on parade
In lavish musicals he made.
When these big movies first came out
His genius was not in doubt:
Jesus Christ Superstar was proof
And so was *Fiddler on the Roof.*

He came back home in '78,
To his Ontario estate.
Far from the film world's tittle-tattle,
His farm made syrup and bred cattle.

Still frequently he travelled down
To work in films in Tinseltown,
But he insisted that his role
Should give him now much more control.

His *Moonstruck* was one great success
With three Academy Awards, no less!

Though trophies and awards abounded
The new Film Centre which he founded
Gave him the greatest pride of all.
It fosters those who hear the call
To learn the art at which he shone:
The art of Norman Jewison.

JACQUES PLANTE
1929 – 1986

*(Jacques Plante grew up, the eldest of eleven children,
in Shawninigan, Quebec, and became a star hockey player with
Les Canadiens in Montreal. The injuries he suffered as a goal
keeper led him to invent a mask to protect his head and face.
Ridiculed at first, his mask developed into the regulation
headgear worn by all goalies today)*

As Jacques grew up, he had the wit
To learn to cook and sew and knit –
Talents that stood him in good stead
For the career that lay ahead.

In early games he would appear
Dressed in his knitted home-made gear,
And all through his career he'd sit
In the team dressing-room and knit.
He always said that this ability
Gave to his hands their flexibility.

His play too was unorthodox
And gave his coaches many shocks,
For as a goalie he would get
Both outside and behind the net.

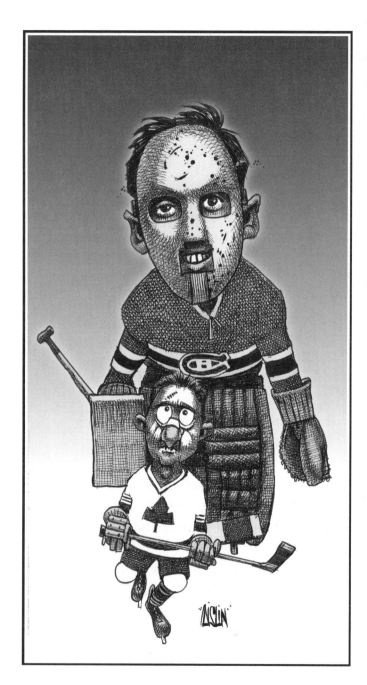

The press who watched the moves he'd make
Gave him the nickname *Jake the Snake*.

A goalie's life is full of risk:
The puck, that hurtling rubber disk
Can make, when at full speed it's sent
A truly devastating dent.

Jacques, as he made his daring dashes,
Had got a lot of gory gashes.
His fortitude was much admired:
Two hundred stitches he acquired.

So Jacques decided he'd devise
A mask to shield his face and eyes.
It looked, although it worked just fine,
Like something made by Frankenstein.
He didn't care, but wore the thing
Each time the team was practising.

Then one night, playing the New York Rangers,
Jacques thought he'd faced too many dangers
When a deep gash across his nose
Took seven stitches more to close.
He said: "I'll not go back out there
Unless I have my mask to wear."

Although the fans might point and grin,
Jacques and his team went on to win.
They won that game and many more
And Jacques kept on the mask he wore.

The coach might fume and fret about it
But Jacques would never play without it.
The coach stopped saying: "Give it up!"
The day they won the Stanley Cup.

The mask that was Jacques Plante's invention
Is now a regular convention.
And Jacques, with *les Canadiens*,
Could say: *"Je ne regrette rien!"*

CHRISTOPHER PLUMMER
(Born 1929)

*(Born in Toronto, Christopher Plummer went to school in Montreal
and then made his first professional appearance in Ottawa in 1950.
He went on to become one of Canada's most celebrated actors, and
to win international acclaim and many awards)*

His smart friends told Christopher Plummer:
"You'll never succeed as a mummer!"
    But he didn't take long
    To prove them all wrong –
His success struck them dumb, if not dumber!

At three Stratfords his welcome was warm –
Connecticut first showed his form;
    He had them all ravin'
    At Stratford-on-Avon
And took our own Stratford by storm.

After Christopher Plummer had starred
In so many plays by the Bard
    He'd no problem being seen
    On the cinema screen:
Even *Star Trek* he didn't find hard.

He sang too, in several shows:
In *Cyrano*, he sang through his nose.
    Sound of Music was nice
    When he crooned *Edelweiss*
To his children up there in the snows.

He's had the most busy of lives
With films, theatre, TV – and three wives;
    But he still treads the boards
    And collects more awards
As for further success he still strives.

The part of John Barrymore made
A great one-man show that he played.
    As Best Actor he scored
    With a Tony Award
The Theatre's most proud accolade.

MORDECAI RICHLER
(1931 – 2001)

*(Mordecai Richler's grandfather came to Canada to escape the
pogroms in Russia, and settled in Montreal where Mordecai grew
up. He used the world of his childhood as a background in a number
of his novels, and these and his other books displayed his talent for
creating characters as well as his brilliant satirical wit. This he also
used with great effect in the cultural battles of French Canada)*

Mordecai lived on St. Urbain
Where his grandfather came, full of hope.
It was largely a Jewish community
Though the street was named after a Pope.

He built castles of snow for mock battles
With the rest of the kids on the block.
They used pieces of coal to play hockey
And for football, a sawdust-filled sock.

The kids would debate cosmic questions:
Would you score if you took Spanish Fly?
Why did Tarzan not go to the toilet?
Did Superman go in the sky?

But this place with its close web of families
And characters he would recall
Gave Richler rich sources for stories,
Duddy Kravitz the richest of all.

Richler departed for Europe
And managed to live by his pen.
He developed his talent for satire
In the style of the Angry Young Men.

He attacked the ex-pats and their poses
And Hollywood wasn't ignored:
Cocksure with its bawdy belligerence
Won a Governor General's Award.

He'd another for *St. Urbain's Horseman*,
The giant who gave evil short shrift,
And critics, delighted with Richler,
Compared him to Kafka and Swift.

Then he took on the family saga
In *Solomon Gursky Was Here*;
He caricatured several icons
And some myths that Canadians hold dear.

Now Richler enjoyed his persona
As a satirist, savage and wry.
He liked to be thought controversial –
It meant that his profile stayed high.

Then he mocked at the new regulations
Which Quebec thought were on the right lines
Restricting the uses of English
On advertisements, posters and signs.

His attack angered some French Canadians
Whose fury lashed out without stint.
For months the row raged around Richler
And occupied pages of print.

In his life and his work he was searching
And trying to explore through and through
The nature of Jewish identity
And that of Canadians too.

However he railed at society
And was railed at in turn for his gall,
He always declared he'd live nowhere
Except his home town, Montreal.

1934 - 2002

PETER GZOWSKI
(1934 – 2002)

*(Born in Galt, Ontario, Peter Gzowski went to the University
of Toronto where as editor of* Varsity News *he developed a passion
for journalism, and abandoned his studies for work in a series
of small town papers. His career moved at a hectic pace and he
was managing editor of* Maclean's *while still in his twenties.
When he moved to CBC Radio his unique, engaging style as a
talk-show host brought him a nationwide audience in a
radio career that spanned more than a quarter of a century)*

Tiring of the quest for knowledge
Peter dropped right out of college,
Saying: "It's too dull for me!"
(But in spite of such perversity,
Later on, the University
Gave him an honorary degree.)

Small towns were his first scenario –
Saskatchewan and then Ontario
Were his journalistic beat.
He admired their local pride
And he soon identified
With the people he would meet.

Now *Maclean's* was soon inviting
Peter Gzowski to be writing
And the readers thought him great.
Caring, eloquent and clever,
He became the youngest ever
Editor, at twenty-eight.

Then *This Country in the Morning*
Marked the debut and the dawning
Of his radio career.
Everyone could hear how that show
Revolutionized the Chat Show –
Gzowski was the pioneer.

Soon his warmth and curiosity,
Questions asked without ferocity,
Made his show the listeners' choice.
Morningside throughout the nation
Really made the reputation
Of that smoky, mellow voice.

To the meek and to the mighty,
The shy, the feckless and the flighty,
He would talk with equal zest.
Dalton Camp and Margaret Atwood,
Anyone who loved to chat would
Clamour to be Gzowski's guest.

Ordinary lives enthralled him,
"Favourite Uncle" many called him:
When he spoke he seemed to smile.
Off the air, his personality
Showed a bit less geniality
With a gruff, dismissive style.

But with spiky moustache twitching
As the questions he was pitching,
Gzowski was the nation's pet.
He loved to golf and loved to gamble –
Into pool rooms he would amble
Always looking for a bet.

He made his show kaleidoscopic,
Tackling each Canadian topic
With a sense of national unity.
With self-confident elation
Gzowski made the declaration:
"Canada is my community."

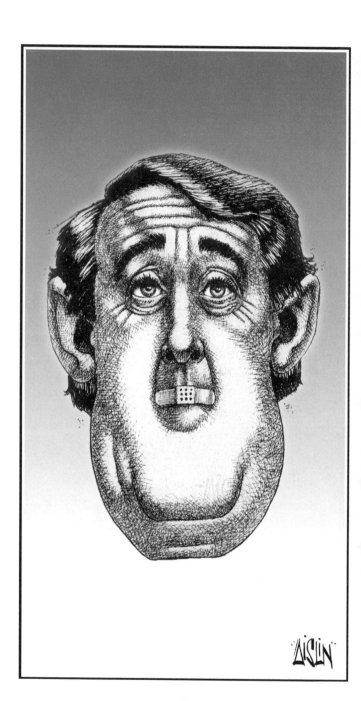

BRIAN MULRONEY
(Born 1939)

(Born in Baie-Comeau, Quebec, where his Irish immigrant
father worked as an electrician in the paper mill, Brian Mulroney
got involved with Conservative politics as a student at
St. Francis Xavier University in Nova Scotia. He returned to
Quebec to take a law degree at Laval, and to become a key figure
in the party. He went on to lead the Progressive Conservatives
to their record-breaking victory in 1984)

He was an electrician's son –
Mulroney was his name.
He wanted to be Number One
And stake his claim to fame.

For power and prestige he yearned
And at St. Francis Xavier
With glad hands and with smiles he learned
Political behaviour.

He courted all of the elite
Whose praise he hoped to win
And everywhere, they seemed to meet
That formidable chin.

That long profile was also high:
He flourished at the Bar;
The Cliche Commission by and by
Made Brian a rising star.

He'd never deigned to try the test
Of ordinary election –
Yet he decided he'd contest
The leadership selection.

Some thought it brave, some thought it brash,
But Brian went on with patience
And with the help of lots of cash
From corporate donations.

He failed, but later on that quest
Once more he would embark.
This time his colleagues were impressed:
Mulroney beat Joe Clark.

Just one year later Brian was proud
To claim his finest hour.
Big Business cheered long and loud:
The Tories were in power!

With tycoons Brian was in cahoots,
The businessman's Prime Minister.
It wasn't just his taste in suits
That Liberals found sinister.

The nation he would soon divide
As Liberal tempers frayed
When resolutely Brian tried
To introduce Free Trade.

He sang with Reagan and with Bush
To get towards his goals,
And then he made the final push
And triumphed at the polls.

Another goal he tried to reach
Was sorting out Quebec;
He sailed upon the Lake of Meech
But found a slippery deck.

Not all of the provincial crew
Agreed to stay on board.
Said Brian: "Instead I'll bring to you
The Charlottetown Accord!"

A referendum then said No;
Quebec toyed with secession.
Brian's popularity was low
Because of the recession.

And what with that, and GST,
His status on the slide,
Mulroney said: "It's time for me
Perhaps to step aside."

Kim Campbell was the one he'd tip –
Was there a hint of malice?
She found the Tory leadership
To be a poisoned chalice.

Tories hailed Brian as P.M.
In 1984;
His leadership had given them
Two hundred seats and more.

But now in 1993
Conservatives were mad:
The outcome was calamity –
Two seats were all they had!

With Brian, the party's rise and fall
Had both been meteoric,
But he was certain, most of all,
His reign had been historic.

He said: "The Liberals' secret is
Quite easy to divine:
They've just adopted policies
Identical to mine!"

CONRAD BLACK
(Born 1944)

*(Born in Montreal, Conrad Black showed early commercial
expertise, even as a schoolboy. He went on to use this talent with
skill and shrewdness to become one of the world's biggest
newspaper tycoons, and to attract both admiration and controversy
in pursuit of his financial, political and social ambitions)*

"The journalist," said Conrad Black
"Is nothing but a lazy hack,
A grunting jackal, overrated,
Dishonest and opinionated."

A view which makes us quite surprised:
We wonder, if he so despised
The journalists and all their capers,
Why did he buy so many papers?

When Conrad was a boy of eight
He thought the stock market was great,
Saved sixty dollars up with care
And bought one General Motors share.

Even in school, at just fifteen,
His keen commercial flair was seen.

Having obtained, by happy chance,
Some question papers in advance,
He sold them to his fellow-students –
A clever scheme, but lacking prudence,
For when discovered, Conrad Black
Was promptly told to go and pack.

Was he convinced by this rash sortie
That selling papers was his forte?

His empire-building started small
In Knowlton, just near Montreal.
He bought, being wise and growing wiser,
The Eastern Townships Advertiser.

Then other papers in Quebec
Began a wave that none could check.
His skilful tactics, it was plain
Were like a military campaign;
For Conrad's hero from the start
Had been Napoleon Bonaparte.

His strategy was far from gentle
And totally unsentimental:
When once a paper was acquired
A number of the staff were fired,
And then he'd look with gaze intense
At every item of expense.

For in this journalistic game
Making a profit was his aim –
And Conrad Black succeeded too,
As round the world his empire grew.

In Canada the power he'd wield
Saw firms and corporations yield.
Soon each new title that he'd buy
Would start a fretful hue and cry.
People would ask: "As he expands
Is too much power in his hands?"

Meanwhile, throughout the U.S.A.
Dozens of papers came his way;
He strutted the Australian stage
With the prestigious *Melbourne Age*.
Even in Israel he could boast
Of getting the *Jerusalem Post*.

But English bigwigs didn't laugh
When he acquired the *Telegraph* –
And neither did the paper's staff.
For soon, because of Conrad Black
Two-thirds of them had got the sack.

His wife, however, he'd enlist
To air her view as columnist.

A view he praises, since it is
Just as conservative as his.

He made the circulation soar
Up to a million and more,
Which furthered Conrad Black's intent
To enter the Establishment.

And soon the ranks of Those Who Mattered
Around his dinner table chattered.
Margaret Thatcher was impressed:
Now Conrad Black had passed the test.

He always used to preen and smile
When dressed up in flamboyant style,
And when the Queen he once escorted
A military rig he sported.
He partied too, in fancy dress,
Clad as a cardinal, no less.

Of all sartorial rewards
Nothing could match the House of Lords:
Given a peerage, he'd determine
To find the richest robes and ermine.

It made the Lords and Ladies swoon:
One more Canadian tycoon!

First Beaverbrook, then Thomson – now
Lord Conrad Black would take a bow.

He had achieved his great ambition
For wealth, and power – and Recognition;
Which shows what grandeur and what gains
Are fashioned out of paper chains.

NEIL YOUNG
(Born 1945)

*(Born in Toronto, Neil Young grew up there and in Winnipeg,
where he soon displayed his talent for music in local groups. He
moved back to Toronto and then decided to try his luck on the rock
scene in California. With many tours and many bands and albums,
he made his name as the rock superstar he remains today)*

As a child, Neil practised daily
Upon his plastic ukelele
Dreaming as he'd pluck and strum
Of the starry times to come.

In high school bands he got the chance
To play at many a teenage dance.
Then when he was just nineteen
He moved to the Toronto scene.

Bruce Palmer met him there, he said,
An amplifier on his head.
(Then and since, Neil's had the feeling
That eccentricity's appealing).
With Palmer's *Mynah Birds* he played
And a big impression made.

THE LATEST CD FROM...

Neil Young

Well, umm, actually
Neil Older-But-Wiser

But then a Motown record start
Came to grief and fell apart.
Back home, Neil felt the future lay
Far westwards, in the U.S.A.

And so to fund this new career
He and Bruce Palmer pawned their gear,
And then with money in their purse
They bought an ancient Pontiac hearse.

They put in it, to help them cope,
Two girl friends and guitars and dope
And feeling happy, high and hip
Ready for every kind of trip
They crossed into the U.S.A.
And finally they reached L.A.

After tough times and unpaid bills
They met again with Stephen Stills
And from that group a new band came:
Buffalo Springfield was its name.
(The name in actual fact had been
On a steam roller they had seen).

Their act on stage saw Stills appear
Dressed up in fancy cowboy gear;
Neil Young his image would assert
By donning a Comanche shirt.

Both, certain of their roles as stars,
Duelled musically with their guitars;
And there were times of wrath and rage
They wielded them in duels backstage.

Neil's huge career had now begun:
The world of rock he soon would stun
Sometimes with groups, sometimes alone
With solo albums of his own.

With great success he'd played and sung
With Crosby, Stills and Nash and Young.
Chicago was their first live gig –
At Woodstock then they went down big.

Neil stood out always with a style
That showed how he was versatile.
His folk-rock songs were something new,
Sometimes romantic, sometimes blue –
He'd go for electronics too,
Or country, or a touch of soul,
And always, driving rock and roll.

With many different bands he links:
Stray Gators, and the Shocking Pinks,
HORDE and Bluenotes, and of course
His own ensemble, Crazy Horse.

Hundreds of songs Neil Young has penned –
The list it seems will never end.
The love songs, such as *Harvest Moon*;
Differently, that haunting tune.
Songs of regret: *Helpless* was one –
The Needle and the *Damage Done*,
Stringman, and *Long May You Run*.

Long may he run with his success,
Canadian Superstar, no less.
"There ain't no way" – he tells us so –
"I'm gonna let the good times go."

TERRY FOX
(1958 – 1981)

(Born in Winnipeg and brought up in Port Coquitlam, BC,
Terry Fox was only eighteen when his right leg had to be
amputated because of bone cancer. Watching the suffering of his
fellow cancer patients, he determined to raise funds for research to
help conquer the disease. So began his Marathon of Hope,
which continues to be run annually in his honour and has
raised over $300 million dollars worldwide)

School friends might have said of Terry
Basketball was not his scene.
In a team of nineteen players
He was rated just Nineteen.

Yet he aimed for sporting prowess
And a brilliant career;
And when Terry graduated
He was Athlete of the Year.

That career was cruelly shortened –
With the operation done
And his right leg amputated
How could Terry hope to run?

Terry Fox would not be beaten
And he planned a daunting test:
He would run across the country,
Every mile from east to west.

After months of painful training,
Sponsors wondered, could he cope?
In St. John's, they watched him starting
On his Marathon of Hope.

Terry, standing by the harbour,
Dipped his new leg in the tide.
To another distant ocean
He was sure he'd make it stride.

With his boyhood friend Doug Alward
There behind him in the van
Terry Fox's epic journey
Over Newfoundland began.

Newfoundland, then Nova Scotia
And Prince Edward Island too –
Everywhere the crowds would gather,
Urge him on and cheer him through.

In the dark, before the sunrise,
Every day they woke at four.
Every day saw Terry running
Twenty gruelling miles and more.

Those who came to watch him running
With his clumping step-and-hop,
Wondered how he kept on going
On and on without a stop.

Running with his legs uncovered
Even in the freezing rain,
Even when his leg-stump, bleeding,
Made him clench his fists in pain.

The Marathon of Hope went onward
And although it gave him fame,
Raising funds for treating cancer,
That was Terry's only aim.

As he passed them, there were people
Pressing dollars in his hand.
There were gifts, and cash collected
From each corner of the land.

Through Quebec and through Ontario,
Through the storms and heat he passed.
Then near Thunder Bay, he wondered
If this mile would be his last.

Doctors found the cancer spreading –
Terry now could hardly stand.
There could be no happy ending
For the marathon he planned.

Many thousands wept in mourning
When they learned that he was gone.
Terry Fox's fight had ended –
But his Marathon goes on.

k.d. lang
(born 1961)

*(Kathy Lang, the youngest of four children, grew up in
Consort, Alberta and was a brilliant volleyball player at
high school there. When she started her singing career,
her stage antics, eccentric dress and powerful voice gained her
a growing number of fans and some critics. But her style
and personality eventually made her an international star,
as well as a gay icon when she came out as a lesbian)*

She was a Big Boned Gal from southern Alberta
And they loved the way she sang.
She wore cowboy boots and her hair was spiky
And they called her k.d. lang.

A tomboy child in southern Alberta
She shone at volleyball.
Her idol was Maria in *Sound of Music*
But that sound began to pall.

So Kathy launched out into country music
And her star began to shine:
She believed, she said, in reincarnation
And she was Patsy Cline.

She stomped the stage like a singing dervish
And danced on the tables too
While she sang of a *Trail of Broken Hearts*
And *Big Big Love for You.*

All the Nashville fans went crazy for k.d.
Their Wild Alberta Rose,
But her image made uptight radio producers
Ban her records from their shows.

She turned her back on country music
And invented herself anew.
With jazzy songs she was a big sensation
On her album *Ingenue.*

k.d. was the pride of southern Alberta
But she says just what she thinks:
She joined the Animal Rights campaigners
And told the world: "Meat Stinks!"

There was rage among the cattlemen of southern Alberta –
She made them roar and shout.
But there was even more of a shock in store
When k.d. lang came out.

The Gay Rights movement was really ecstatic,
Alberta's government not so sure.

But thousands of fans came along to cheer her
When she made an international tour.

She's won stacks of Grammys and Junos and Tonys,
She's the pride of lesbian chic,
And the world agrees that as a superstar singer
k.d. lang's unique.

THE MONARCH BUTTERFLY

South of the Border,
Down Mexico way,
    There is a butterfly
    That will flutter by
For a holiday.

It stays for the winter
Then flies off one day
Two thousand miles northward
Up Canada way.

Onwards and onwards
They fly on their way
    Till with great relief
    They see the Maple Leaf
And they shout *Hooray*!

Through Canada's summer
They flutter and play
Till it's time to be flying
Down Mexico way.

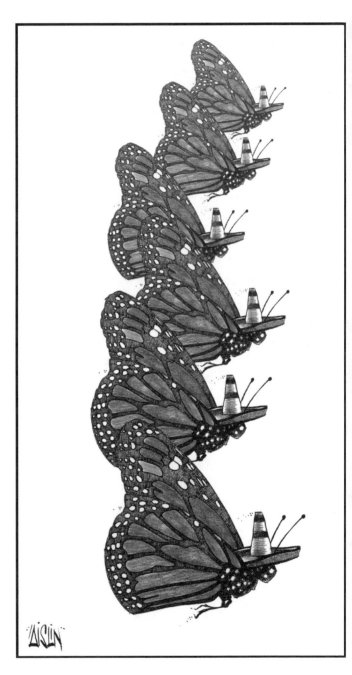

To the very same trees they go flying
On the very same route through the sky
And though butterfly experts keep trying
They can't understand how or why!

A hundred mile journey
It flies in a day
    Danaus Plexippus
    Is perplexing us
Though we cry *Olé*!

So long live the Monarch –
Come back and don't stay
South of the Border
Down Mexico way.

AUTHOR'S NOTE

Once more it has been my great pleasure to work with Aislin on this new verse collection of Canadians past and present which adds to the gallery of remarkable characters featured in our first three books and in the *Oh, Canadians! Omnibus*. They demonstrate yet again the diversity and vitality of Canadians in the arts, politics, sport and science – and we even pay tribute to a dog and a butterfly too.

I would like to thank the London Library, the Canadian Embassy in Dublin, and my good friends Leonard and Joan Ryan, for all their great help with my research.

I am also grateful to Marsha Boulton and her excellent biographies in the *Just a Minute* series.

Aislin has surpassed himself with further perceptive and hilarious illustrations, and I want to thank Mary Hughson for her expert design and production work on the book.

Finally, none of these books would exist without our dynamic publisher Kim McArthur, who has inspired us as ever with her delight, enthusiasm and constant encouragement.

Gordon Snell

CARTOONIST'S NOTE

Gordon Snell, who was born in Singapore, raised in Australia, established a career in London, and presently lives in Dublin, has this inexplicable love affair going on with all things Canadian; and we're glad he does! It is always such a pleasure working with him.

My thanks also to two invaluable allies here at *The Gazette* in Montreal: Pat Duggan and Gaëtan Côté.

Aislin